The First Risk

The First Risk

Charles Jensen

Lethe Press
Maple Shade, NJ

Copyright © 2009 by Charles Jensen. All rights reserved. No part of this book may be reproduced in any form, except for brief citation or review, without the written permission of Lethe Press. For information write: Lethe Press, 118 Heritage Avenue, Maple Shade, NJ 08052.

www.lethepressbooks.com
lethepress@aol.com

Printed in the United States of America
Book Design by Toby Johnson
Cover photography by Kris Sanford
Published as a trade paperback original
by Lethe Press, 118 Heritage Avenue, Maple Shade, NJ 08052.

ISBN 1-59021-217-7 / 978-1-59021-217-2

The First Risk

Acknowledgments

I would to thank the editors of the following magazines, in which these poems first appeared, sometimes in slightly different form:

Bethesda. "Venus Is Haunted by the Death of Adonis."

Columbia Poetry Review. "Venus at the Body of Adonis."

Copper Nickel. "V. On Feminine Artifice," "Storyboard II," "IV. Notes on Casting, Vertigo," "Producer's Note on the Rushes," "VIII. The Machinations of Gender," "Storyboard III," "X. Pathetic Masculinity and the Desire to Possess," "Director's Note, Scene 133"

Court Green. "Barcelona, City of the Sad Divas."

Hayden's Ferry Review: Selections from "Safe": "[I recognize his face through all the dried blood.]," "[That October we both wore braces on our teeth—]," "[A man and a gun walk into a bar.]," "I could not have held him, pulled him from the fence]"

The Journal. "La Agrado Explains Plastic Surgery," "La Agrado's Catalog of Ills"

Knockout: Selections from "Safe": "[He takes a limousine due south]," "[In the night I was desperate to be cradled]," "[How should I live with this knowledge]," "Storyboard I," and "Storyboard IV."

Libro Libre A Casa Libre Anthology. "*Introduction:* On Vertigo," "II. The Dissemination of Knowledge," "A. INT—SAN FRANCISCO—NIGHT," "III. Meconaissance," "A. Wardrobe Notes, Scene 68"

MiPoesias: "I Am the Boy Who Is Tied Down"

No Tell Motel. "The Field, Barcelona," "Nina," "Nina (2)," "Huma Rojo," "Huma Rojo (2)"

OCHO. "It Was October," Selections from "Safe": "[He goes into the truck]," "A gun has ownership over the hand, caresses the palm in such a way]." "As the night inked in above the mountains in a slow hand, could he recognize time:]," "[The skin's an ignoble thing until touched or town—]," "[I believed we were safe before he died]."

PISTOLA. "Venus Arrives at the Body of Adonis," "In Laramie."

spork. "Documentation of Edward Dixon's First Attempt to Reach the Ghost-World: November 1934," Entry: Edward Dixon's Diary (October 6, 1943)," "Shredded Document Recovered from the Dixon Papers, Reassembled January 2006 (2)," "Edward Dixon's Subsequent Attempts to Reach the Ghost-World Were Unsuccessful," "Shredded Document Recovered from the Dixon Papers, Reassembled January 2006 (3)," "Shredded Document Recovered from the Dixon Papers, Reassembled January 2006 (5)"

Willow Springs: Selections from "Safe": "[At twenty-one I hated my body]" and "[He goes into the field. The headlights form two straight lanes]"

The Strange Case of Maribel Dixon was published in its entirety as a chapbook by New Michigan Press in 2007.

I would like to extend gratitude to friends and colleagues who read this manuscript in various forms and provided helpful insight: Christopher Hennessy, Tom Wayman, and Jeremy Halinen. Special thanks are in order for Stephanie Lenox, whose support was instrumental in assembling this manuscript.

I am also grateful to the Arizona Commission on the Arts for an Artist's Project Grant that made completion of this work possible, and to Casa Libre en la Solana for a residency that provided time and space in which to complete these poems.

"Safe" is in memory of Matthew Shepard. "The Strange Case of Maribel Dixon" is for Robert Blair.

Contents

I. Safe

It Was October 2
    Venus Arrives at the Body of Adonis 3
In Laramie 4
    Venus at the Body of Adonis 5
I Am the Boy Who Is Tied Down 6
    Venus Is Haunted by the Death of Adonis 9
Safe 10

II. City Of The Sad Divas

Manuela Grieves 24
La Agrado Explains Plastic Surgery 25
The Field, Barcelona 26
Nina Explains Heroin 28
Huma Rojo Recalls the Boy 29
Diversons 30
Nina Leaves Her 31
Huma Rojo Grieves 32
La Agrado's Catalog of Ills 33
Manuela Returns to Barcelona 34
The Beating of La Agrado 35
Barcelona, City of the Sad Divas 36

III. The Double Bind: A Critical Text

I.   Introduction: On *Vertigo* / INT—SAN FRANCISCO HOTEL—NIGHT 39
II.   Meconaissance / Wardrobe Notes, Scene 68 41
III. The Two Films in *Vertigo* / Storyboard I 43
IV. On Feminine Artifice / Storyboard II 45
V.   Notes on Casting, *Vertigo* / Producer's Notes on the Rushes 47
VI. Obsession in the Films of Alfred Hitchcock / Hair and Make-up Notes, Scene 92 49
VII. The Machinations of Gender / Storyboard III 51

VIII.	The Mobility of Feminine Identity / Storyboard IV	53
IX.	"Pathetic Masculinity" and the Desire to Possess / Director's Notes, Scene 133	55

IV. The Strange Case Of Maribel Dixon

Preface: Excerpt from Edward Dixon's Thesis Manuscript *Manifestations of Metaphysical Energy as Biological Entities: Survival within the Ghost-World Dimension*, as Discovered by Graduate Student Researchers Archiving His Papers 59

1. "Documentation of Edward Dixon's First Attempt to Reach the Ghost-World: November, 1934" 60
    - 1a. Entry: Edward Dixon's Diary (October 6, 1943) 61
    - 1b. Shredded Document Recovered from the Dixon Papers, Reassembled January 2006 (1) 62
    - 1c. Entry: Edward Dixon's Diary (April 22, 1954) 63

2. "Maribel Vanishes, November 1934" 64
    - 2a. Shredded Document Recovered from the Dixon Papers, Reassembled January 2006 (2) 65
    - 2b. Entry: Edward Dixon's Diary (July 17, 1937) 67

3. "Edward Dixon's Subsequent Attempts to Reach the Ghost-World Were Unsuccessful" 68
    - 3a. Shredded Document Recovered from the Dixon Papers, Reassembled January 2006 (3) 69
    - 3b. Entry: Edward Dixon's Diary (December 14, 1960) 71
    - 3c. Shredded Document Recovered from the Dixon Papers, Reassembled January 2006 (4) 72

4. "Edward Dixon, the Recluse" 73
    - 4a. Entry: Edward Dixon's Diary (May 21, 1974) 74
    - 4b. Document 729: Singed Fragment Discovered Near Site Of Edward Dixon's Burned Laboratory, Ca 1974 75
    - 4c. Shredded Document Recovered from The Dixon Papers, Reassembled January 2006 (5) 76

I.

Safe

On October 7, 1998, Matthew Shepard was lured from a bar by two men. Kidnapped and driven to the outskirts of Laramie, Wyoming, Matthew was robbed, savagely beaten, and tied to a fence, where he was left to die.

IT WAS OCTOBER

I was love when I entered the bar
shivering in my thin t-shirt and ripped jeans
and I was love when I left that place, tugged along at the wrist
as though tied, with a man I did not know.

I was love there in the morning
when our sour kisses bore the peat of rotten leaves,
fallen October leaves. And it was love that we kissed anyway, not knowing
each other's names.

I was love in that bed
and I was love in the hall and down the stairs and into the freezing rain.

I was love with hands punched deep
into the pockets of a coat.
I was love coated in frozen rain.

Back home, I was love stripped of the cigarette-stung shirt, love pulling the stiff jeans from my legs.
I dried my hair and I was love.

It was October. What did I know of love that year,
shuddering in my nervous skin. Miles away, the boy was lashed to a fence and shivering.

Where that place turned red and the ground soaked through
with what he was, I was love.

What did I know of love then
but that it wasn't enough.

VENUS ARRIVES AT THE BODY OF ADONIS

Detail from Luca Cambiaso's "Death of Adonis" (ca. 1570)

She leans near his lips
to capture his last breaths—

each one a small secret she'll keep safe
the only place she can:

her perfect body.
She defines his mortality in theoretical terms—

what death is
has no value to her. She lives on.

Crouched over his body in the field,
she might believe

despite her flawless form and endless breath
death divides the mortals from the gods—

now she understands
how love, its curse

makes a mortal of her, or something like.

IN LARAMIE

*I'll keep loving all I'm given to
love, there's no other revenge.*
— Christopher Davis

The body is
taken from the roadside strap.

The hewn ties
knotted at the wrists are the worst kind of lie:

the body
of the boy has been removed from its post

like a sandbag,
heavy and limp, clotted with bits of dried grass.

I lay him
across my lap.

I stroke
his blood-soaked hair with my cold hand.

He smells
not human, but machine—the copper of his body is not alive.

My body,
mechanical in its care of him, shudders like clockwork gears, but

I'll keep loving
all I'm given. There's no other gift.

The boy
is taken from my arms. There's no revenge for losing this,

no mistake.
There's no remaking what is lost, and yes—

there's
no other love.

VENUS AT THE BODY OF ADONIS

Detail from Luca Cambiaso's "Death of Adonis" (ca. 1570)

In the field,
she stutters a few crooked words—useless.

No one hears.
The silence wraps her in a wet shawl, the humid dusk.

His body is
red. His legs—hard as felled timbers—no longer needed.

She observes
how simple this reduction is: his skin slowly cools

like fresh bread.
The familiar smell of his sweat, robust and sharp

begins to dry.
She is the only one who will notice this

simple loss.
The shawl closes her in until her breath

breaks free
of the field as fog. She observes loss like a foreign language:

as lame as white noise.
She places her cold hand on his cold skin. She takes in the air

but he is not in it.
She sees now she was doomed to love him this way,

that loss is the smallest currency
of loving.

I AM THE BOY WHO IS TIED DOWN

I am the boy who is tied down.

        I am the moon. A boy is tied down to a fence by his wrists
        while two boys look on.

        Sky bears down on the landscape like an open mouth.
        The mountains sink into the earth. Shards of broken teeth.

    I am the smooth mahogany bar on which the boy's small hands rest.
        I stretch out as the bartender lowers his head,
        washing glasses.

            I am a combustion engine and each of my pistons starts
            a fire. Laden with boys who trek out of town

            toward a nothingness of dirt roads.

I am the mind of a killer. I carry a gun in the boy's hand and like a puppeteer
I tell the boy what to say.

                I am a bone of the body. Every seven years
                I am completely new and have no memory
                of what came before. If I am broken, I grow back.
                    If I am shattered, the body absorbs me
                        or dies.

I am the boy tied to a fence and I have a deep wound for the world.

I am the night. I have more stars than there are names;
if I listed them here you would forget them or move on.
     The night is not conventional time. In the darkness I know
you are capable of so much, so much.

I am the rescue. I swoop in, wordless, detached. I am things taken apart.
    I am the split of the rail and the rise of the body toward the light.
    I am the smell of blood.

                    I swoop in, wordless, detached.

       I am the body and the wreck.

                    I am the failure of the body to remain a boy.
                    I am the remains of a boy, the body of his failure.

I am the field where the boy died, where he ruined the grass
    with his body and its blood. The body is a heavy thing.
    It is given to me.
        I take it in.

                    I am the connection among all things.

       I am the alpha and omega, the dawn and its darkness, the beginning and the end.

I am a boy driving a pick-up truck out of town. There is only one way to go.
    I drive two boys out of town to its edge, where fences mark the boundaries of
    ranchers' lands. I stop the truck.

Dust settles around us as I lead the boys out.

I am a killer. My hands are two big guns fully loaded.
I am a killer and I go into the night with a pair of hands that fire off shots.
    I smack him with the gun.
    I smack him with the gun.
    I smack him with the gun.

    I am the motion of the head pistol-whipped.
    The force of the blow creates equal, opposite reactions.

I am canals of blood
shunted out through the porous body, open and torn.
    I am the brightness of pain, the loss of breath.

I am the white rejection of the world and the prayer of its vanishing.

I am the noises of the boy
choking on his own blood.

    I am the day before the boy is taken from the bar.

I am the last safe thought he had.

    I am a mess of stars, so careless, continuing to appear.

I am the boy who is tied down.

    I am the path from the truck to the fence, the body of the boy
pushed down, picked up, pushed down.
    I am the halving of this distance,
    the half of that, the half of that.
I refuse to let the boy reach the fence.

VENUS IS HAUNTED BY THE DEATH OF ADONIS

Detail from Luca Cambiaso's "Venus and Adonis" (ca. 1565)

She watches him killed again and again
with filmic precision. Her eyelids flutter and move—

butterfly shutters parse light, snap time into frames
and freeze him like this—like this—like this.

In a series of stills, his lips turn red to blue.

The wild boar's tusks dig into his flesh. Like his
heart is a forgetful thing with nothing to prove.
It forgets her face, forgets to beat on.

No matter what happens,
night slips over the world
like a glove. The night bears a gun like this

dream: She swoops down from the sky
as if he could be saved. The dawn comes on
like blind rage, white and searing;

his body sputters, skin goes numb.
Too easily his mortal lungs give up,

give in, give his breath one last shove
like this—like this—like this—

SAFE

Fact will muzzle anything.
—Matthea Harvey

He goes into the truck
and all over town, faces pulled from the fray

iris out into pinprick holes in dark drapes, into windows and door frames
The sky blacks out

until it bears out its sad shroud
Small pairs of stars appear from horizon to horizon, blinking

The boys roll straight into black
three bullets shy

I recognize his face through all the dried blood. They say
the skin showed through only where his tears ran down

and it means all through the night
he felt pain

To reduce this down to its most intimate parts
is all I want to do

his red face
streaked with skin

He goes into the field. The headlights form two straight lanes
through the grass and in their white glow, three faces blanch. Backlit with darkening haloes

The fence's thin spine cracks through the buckled landscape
Moths bat themselves against the truck's fender. They think it's the light of the moon

A tragic misrecognition. These small confusions wear us down
He shields his face from the first blow. Eventually his hands drop

The moths keep beating their furred heads against the light
They want to go into the light. They want to be engulfed by light

The body only wants to touch another body. To share heat
which must be conserved

His lips torn to shreds against each steady blow
the very same night mine opened against a kiss, the rasp and burn of beard rash

and my breath, too, left me in quick, shallow bursts
as though punched in the gut

If hate craves blood and blood craves a body
we are simply helpless

A gun has ownership over the hand, caresses the palm in such a way,
speaks a message:

You are a killer
You enter the night as a man and come out red. You come out unshaken—

You come out of the night and someone else won't follow you—someone else has been bloodied
for twenty dollars and a pair of shoes

You are a killer
You came back red

As the night inked in above the mountains in a slow hand, could he recognize time:
could he then see light as it bleached the sky, burned out the stars

or was it
endless

expansive
hollowed out

did it swallow him
or did it chew

How can we live with this knowledge:
that he struggled, that he knew they would kill him, that he begged anyway

that they laughed
and bought cigarettes with his pocket change

I was twenty-one. It was autumn
How are we to live

in this cage of knowing

The hospital bed where he slipped deeper into the field
so tortured any touch brought him to spasm—even his mother's hand

A sky slurred over with a mess of star glitter
and a voice—small, reduced, asking to live—fades

We have come now to a silence
The night is too small

and the pool of blood wets his ear
with its cold tongue

The main street in Laramie rolls out like a long, gray tongue
and it knows

how I taste. It knows my smell
Each night absorbs that old dry road

until only headlights make it real
as the point of a gun

as webbed bone shattering outward
from the skull toward dry, brittle grass

He takes a limousine due south
to the only safe bar he can think of, where touch is less accidental

less apologetic
Away from the blunt noses of firearms. Away from the seam of fences splitting the land

into scarred land—damaged, divisible. There are two lands and one of them needs a scarecrow
shooing off the rest of us. We get the message

There is always a cold field
just a short drive from here

The skin's an ignoble thing until touched or torn—
even the most brutal contact has a shared warmth we can't ignore.

The boys wear the purple hoods of night, their eyes wide and white.
The distances between us breathe too close—they share uncomfortable air, the body's steam

electrified by currents of pain
lit up in the skin

which claws at itself
tearing away from the bone

I believed we were safe before he died

Now I hear the cracking of pistols
in the break of a kiss

The soft, steady moan of the wind
in our lungs as we, entangled, pant

Now the event is inside us,
rank and sour. We carry its sadness like a gene.

II.

City Of The Sad Divas

after Pedro Almodóvar

MANUELA GRIEVES

She is full
of organs.

The liver, which putrefies the skin;
the heart, failing
all who touch it.

The son who died that night
beneath a car,
Manuela's high heels
dashing to the point of impact—

he was once inside her,
a second heart sharing blood.

He lived on her. She equally,
not metaphorically,
lived on him.

LA AGRADO EXPLAINS PLASTIC SURGERY

The body awakens like a sleeper cell
to the secret phrase or melody

that turns it against itself:

loose skin shifts like flags turning
in fickle wind.

Once my body was a boy—
uncomplicated. Smooth eyebrow lines,
full head of hair. Then chaos:

the hair burned off like fog.
Everything lengthened; the hair diffused
all across my body like émigrés.

And later, my disappointment.
I wanted to be more whole, to buy breasts.
I filed my chin down to a delicate nub. I tell you, *chica*,

if you want something done,
do it with a knife.

THE FIELD, BARCELONA

Where you still find cars with dorsal fins,
tail lights glowing cat's-eye thin.

Such circular movements, for so long,
become steps of dance.

Here at the Field, hookers bend forward
on stalks of slender high-heeled boots.

Where love and knives are still
sharing the same breath.

Agrado: she is a waste of good
rhinoplasty. Her eye begins to swell.

The movements of oil derricks in field—
a rocking pump.

Where lipstick smears after blood dries:
money travels light, travels first.

Manuela arrives—a kind of nurse—
shooing men like plague rats.

The smell of body fluid: copper,
bleach. A place of shivered groans.

There is night. There are the hookers
about to drop from their shoes, fake blushes—

at dawn, each man goes home alone,
a snake of taillights uncoiling on the long dirt road.

Manuela arrives—nurse mother, wrenching
some poor high heel from the soft soil.

The girls titter back home, flatten out wads
of crumbled *pesetas* to buy their eggs, maybe a coffee.

NINA EXPLAINS HEROIN

Sometimes it's a wide field like a city avenue—
the horse says sometimes it rides me.

In the sweaty afterlight of dusk, we graze
the same dirty pasture for nuts, berries, good junk.

I offer it a vein. The horse teeth
sting that skin and then it slips right in—

that salty treat. Horse can't get enough of me
with my sweat dried to little crystals

and my need to ride is as insistent as itch,
always unreachable—

As a girl, I watched my uncle's lame horse
blow snot from its nose before he shot it.

White-ringed nose, I screamed, *I'm just a girl*
as trigger snicked back—

I tell my lover, *I'm just a girl* as she
plunges into me where I can't see.

In the doorway, a horse watches. Stamps
its foot. The hollow floor moans, and I moan.

HUMA ROJO RECALLS THE BOY

In Madrid, hounded by autograph seekers, *Drive*,
I say to the taxi. My lover titters like a bird
for her junk. She is barely
in her body: I smell her hover
just above the skin—
copper, tangelos, baby powder—
the smell takes me in a cloud. *Drive*,

I say to the taxi, my lover with black hair.
At the window, in streaks of rain, a boy's face ripples.
He holds a broken pencil. His eyes drip;
her body next to me hums as she slips in,
slips out the membrane of her dry, scaly skin.
Drive, I say. We round the corner—

the night rains hard, dense, a firm hand as it covers
the mouth of a lover. Some seconds later, my bird opens her lips
as the boy's silhouette blocks the headlights—
the screech of tires in that breath; my lover's teeth
grate shrilly down the street like an alley cat
nipping her young by the neck
quick, before they drown.

DIVERSIONS

Manuela, hawk-like, surveys the wide avenue's broken bottles
and there, among rainwater,

gathers pieces to her chest,
things her son dropped in the street—

his notebook,
his thin pencil.

Tonight, she will take in the theatre,
its gaslights and sad divas,
the reliable dialogue, its patrons who
swallow these lies.

NINA LEAVES HER

To be clean
is too easy: letting the danger in,
drinking the tire smoke
for the rip it carves in your throat—

that's love. To go there,
every day, knowing full stop you will be
broken just a little more,

a little more dirt smudged
outside the lips, the blood baking
slightly hotter in its cast-iron vein:

I was never found by a lover.
They only complicate the game, place the safety zone
a little deeper

in the skin. When I shoot up, which of the dimming stars
will be first to nip the desperate bulge
of my vein? That sinking feeling in the gut.

The dirty disappointment my lover wears to find me,
wasted, the flutter of my eyelids kissing junk,
sending their irises to another field.

And the last kiss—
the lip smack breaks us apart.

HUMA ROJO GRIEVES

The beginning of the end
is not a moment but a song: tender notes
you know you've heard before, the sound
a lover makes in her throat
to answer some silly question you've posed—

and the ending comes after
like explosions from far-away fireworks:
delayed, embittered, put out.

And though the lover has her cries—
the one for loving, the one for lonesomeness,
the cry that signals sleep will come, the cry
that coats the body in its low, warm vibration—
the end has no cry; the end

like a tire's slow leak comes with a hiss,
a delicate release giving the body to gravity,
to the ground, before the wound's even felt.

LA AGRADO'S CATALOG OF ILLS

The nose, broken in a beating,
left crooked.

Pattern baldness, wiggle-fat drooped
near the elbows. Sacks lumped near the beaks of the eyes.

Here in the desert of my beauty,
my tumbleweed eyebrows blow under my hair,
must be redrawn again and again.

And there is no rain: my crackled face
opens in a hundred places,

each parched mouth nipping at the dry air
while the rest of the face hardens, practicing for the last look,

the stuck expression looking perfectly wan
under precisely the right lighting.

MANUELA RETURNS TO BARCELONA

She gets lost in wallpaper,
brambles of arabesques a cloying fandango
of melting eyes: she thinks
there's too much orange.

She thinks of Barcelona this way,
Gaudí's balconies limp as a quivering
lower lip. Thirty-five drooping lips
outside the living room window alone,

each one heavy with birds, wet towels,
the arm of a young boy with brown hair.

In the slight breeze that picks up,
she watches trance-like
the way his hair curls like little fingers
saying, *Ven aquí*.

THE BEATING OF LA AGRADO

The body is as resilient
as earth: like earth, the body
is the constant
threat of dust. And destruction is
nothing I ever dreamed:

the beating hands work me through
like plaster and water, warming
slowly at the touch. The hands know

that this can burn. All the notes
I took to my body, those revisions
equal to nothing. A reduction
of terms, the narrowing of the shoulders

toward the thin waist, and lower,
where even more narrow
the hips reduce into feet:

And the nose. The beating of it,
the foster parent fingers kneading it
from a delicate swoop into bonecrush.

BARCELONA, CITY OF THE SAD DIVAS

Where there was a city they placed
a man.

Where the man had invisible breasts,
they placed two breasts.

Where there was mascara, they drew dark irises.

They placed a city in between the two round melons
of the chest where it plunged like a teardrop gemstone.

Where Chanel was sold, they sold
slabs of beef.

They substituted turkey for the beef on Fridays.

Where men felt anxious, they offered
two bee-stung lips for company.

Where men felt abandoned, they offered
torn up pictures of forgotten parents.

They provided salt for every wound, every corner
of the city was ripe with good junk.

Where they offered junk, they substituted
coffee grounds, homemade breakfasts.

Where the city slept, they placed a man.
His breasts overlooked the town like two oppressive churches.

The women of Barcelona, their lined faces
and the pallor, the smoke of living in fumes,

their slippery traces pull in and out of town
where the man is a sharp breath under a doctor's knife.

III.

The Double Bind: A Critical Text

"There are many such stories."
—*Vertigo*

I. INTRODUCTION: ON *VERTIGO*

Hitchcock opens on a chase across San Francisco rooftops. Jimmy Stewart hounds a criminal. Someone unexpected dies and it's more chilling than we care to admit, this small unknowable death that begins the film: a body plummets from the roofs as Stewart clings to the building's drain pipe. And so begins his malady: disequilibrium of the mind inside the body, the perception of a world in constant motion around him.

Stewart hangs by his hands. Hitchcock invented the technique to signify his sudden dizziness: the track-back zoom. The background retreats while the foreground moves closer to the viewer. To do this, Hitchcock used a backward tracking dolly shot coupled with a zoom lens. It cost nineteen thousand dollars in 1957.

Spatial distortion is the hallmark of true vertigo.

INT—SAN FRANCISCO HOTEL—NIGHT.

The neon hotel sign outside your window
beats on and off in time with our breath.

The room we're in goes turquoise,
then rich red.

The sky outside is hollow, full of echoes.
My hand holds your empty hand.

You are like a hotel that has a vacancy:
I want to fill you with me.

II. MECONAISSANCE

Vertigo was widely criticized upon release for revealing the truth too early in the film. Revelation disrupts disbelief. We learn that Madeleine was never Madeleine but that she was Judy, always Judy, in disguise. When Scottie meets Judy and makes her over into Madeleine, he creates a double-bind: Judy as Madeleine-Judy as Judy as Scottie's version of Madeleine.

For some scenes, the second unit was dispatched into San Francisco to film establishing shots and special takes of stand-ins for Jimmy Stewart and Kim Novak. One such scene occurs in the museum, where "Madeleine" stares rapturously into the painting of the mad Carlotta. From this distance, the Novak stand-in is far enough away that, unknowingly, we assume it to be her. The Stewart double never turns fully toward the camera, watching the woman watching the painting. Here the audience takes on Scottie's narrative misrecognitions: a woman made up to be Kim Novak playing Judy appearing to be Madeleine appearing to be haunted by the ghost of Carlotta Valdes. And, too, that this generic stand-in is a facsimile of Jimmy Stewart. Anyone can be anyone.

WARDROBE NOTES, SCENE 68.

In this scene you're telling me
you love me.

Your motivation is to make me believe you—
I want to believe you.

Everything on your body must be perfect:

I'll style your hair,
straighten your tie—

if you forget your lines
I'll paint your lips with every red verb.

III. THE TWO FILMS IN *VERTIGO*

Hitchcock aspired to make two films in *Vertigo*: the first, a conventional narrative film in the vein of his past supernatural thrillers like *Rebecca*; the second, a silent film. Hitchcock's earlier releases were silent. One of his first major films, *The Lodger*, features Ivor Novello as a man determined to discover whether a young male lodger is a Jack the Ripper-like murderer terrorizing London. In *Vertigo*, the desire for truth is still the primary mission: is Madeleine possessed?

The silent aspects of *Vertigo*—where no dialogue can be exchanged—occur as Scottie follows Madeleine about her haunted daily errands: to the flower shop, to the museum, to the guest house, to the Palace of the Legion of Honor. Only Bernard Herrmann's haunting score is heard during these sequences. That, and the image. We are watching him watching her. There is nothing more to be said of it.

STORYBOARD I

There are many such stories:

someone is loved and lost;
the other carries on but is less himself.

The hills of the city shrug close together
as if to say, *So it will be*.

In the film, I splice a frame of your face,
then his face. In high speed you share this face.

IV. ON FEMININE ARTIFICE

The archetypical gray suit Kim Novak wears for much of the film—both as Madeleine and as Judy made over into Madeleine by Scottie—is itself her most haunting attribute. With her white hair and white gloves, all the artifice of her character makes her seem colorless, lifeless—dead already. In the film, Gavin Elster explains his wife is twenty-six years old, and yet in those clothes, with that hair, she appears much older, almost middle aged—closer, too, to her husband's age, who is Scottie's age.

It isn't until Scottie strips her of the suit, after she jumps into San Francisco Bay, that her true age becomes apparent. She is, after all, just a girl. Later, as Judy, her clothes are bright, loud, whorish. Her make-up is clown-like in its garishness. And more than any other aspect, the cut of her dresses in these later scenes makes her appear young and sexual—the opposite of Madeline in every way—making her Madeleine suit even more of a costume, more of a prison.

Kim Novak initially refused to wear gray for the film.

STORYBOARD II

We were nested inside each other
like Russian dolls,

smaller and smaller versions of ourselves
with smaller and smaller hearts.

The brain is all sprockets and gears.
It machines us into being, constant thought.

We shoot day-for-night. Here your body
plummets from the top story of a tall building:

drab green, mustard yellow, Technicolor blue—
FX: a flag flaps; your clothes wind-whipped.

V. NOTES ON CASTING, *VERTIGO*

Hitchcock wanted Vera Miles to play the Kim Novak role. Although he'd never say it, he hated Kim Novak. Vera Miles, with whom he'd work again later in *Psycho* when she played Marion Crane's doggedly determined truth-seeking sister (a role later filled by Julianne Moore in the Gus Van Sant remake), was pregnant. In interviews, Hitchcock implies this was the actress's own irresponsibility and that it alone shut her out of the part. Novak, he insisted, had too many preconceived notions about her role and her characters Judy and Madeleine. In many ways, Novak resisted being made over, being fully made over, into other women.

PRODUCER'S NOTE ON THE RUSHES

I am full
of his scent—gardenias and sandalwood

bloom gracefully in time-lapse.
A blood stain melts outward from the head.

I carry him like this, inside me.
Lilacs crowding the mouth of a small vase.

VI. OBSESSION IN THE FILMS OF ALFRED HITCHCOCK

Hitchcock was said to be obsessed with blonde actresses, and true, it seems more than just coincidence that many of his leading ladies were beautiful blondes: Grace Kelly, Janet Leigh, Tippi Hedren, Joan Fontaine, Carole Lombard, Doris Day.

In *Vertigo*, the true blonde (Barbara Bel Geddes) is overlooked by the platinum glimmer of the phony blonde, the brunette.

His feature films with the most overt homosexual undertones—*Rope* and *Strangers on a Train*—feature only brunettes.

HAIR AND MAKE-UP NOTES, SCENE 92

To be golden-haired means
you are destined to be idolized;

brunettes have less fun
but keep better secrets.

I don't know which you have been
but I know what you will be now.

The truth will always overwhelm
its reconstruction.

VII. THE MACHINATIONS OF GENDER

Vertigo is a film about reducing things down to their most intimate parts. Madeleine, in the end, is just artifice, a kind of machinery—in tribute, perhaps, to the False Maria of Fritz Lang's silent classic *Metropolis*, who is herself a literal machine designed to dupe the male hero into an unfortunate fate.

Scottie's desire to possess Madeleine is also a desire to understand her, to identify what makes her work. After she jumps into the bay and wakes up in Scottie's apartment, she discovers she is naked. She slips into Scottie's robe and walks past the kitchen. Hitchcock keeps the camera focused on the kitchen door, where Scottie has arranged Madeleine's clothing to dry, yet in such a way, it appears he has delicately laid out each piece of her, each disarticulated aspect of her identity, for display. For study.

Later, after Scottie's phone call from Elster, he discovers Madeleine's absence *only because* her various parts and pieces have been removed from the kitchen, reconstituted on her body, and she has vanished.

STORYBOARD III

In this next scene,
you must slice your body open.

Show me how it is that you, the beloved,
are able to function.

Your motivation in this shot
is to reveal to me something I've never known—

surprise me,
a gift, unwrapping yourself

as if you were
the one thing I've ever lacked.

VII. THE MOBILITY OF FEMININE IDENTITY

Midge is another kind of obsession. Scottie's obsession consumes him, owns him, takes him over; he is lost in it. All the while Midge stands by in her obsession with Scottie, loving him, wanting him—being so close to him but never again having him. That she designs undergarments for a living—lingerie, in fact—is a metaphor for her cloaked emotions. They are underneath what she lets Scottie see. And when she paints herself into the portrait of Mad Carlotta, the nesting of female personality is further complicated: Midge is Mad Carlotta is Madeleine is Judy as Madeleine. There is no escape.

Was it fun? Midge wants to know.

Stupid! Stupid! Stupid! she seethes, her hands flattening her hair.

Oh, Johnny, she says.

STORYBOARD IV

In this scene you are determined
to undress yourself,

determined to infatuate.
Remove each item of clothing

as though it were wet with fire,
dripping with fire,

but you love the fire.
Can you give me that?

Understandably, we'll only have
just one take.

IX. "PATHETIC MASCULINITY" AND THE DESIRE TO POSSESS

It is unclear why Scottie's masculinity is constantly questioned in this film—why, for example, his best friend is a woman. Or why the doctor has placed him in a therapeutic support for his back that Scottie and Midge both refer to as a "corset." Or why his bathrobe is soft and delicate, patterned like a woman's. Does Scottie love Madeleine? Is his obsession borne from a desire to possess her, as often is assumed, or is it a desire to *be* her? An oppositional reading of the film reveals an alternative side to Scottie's motives. In dressing up Judy, like a doll, like a little girl, is he in fact displacing his own desire to dress himself up in Madeleine's clothes? Themes like this resurface again and again in the thriller genre in later films like *Dressed to Kill* and *The Silence of the Lambs*.

The desire to possess something—to master it and control it—is the desire to internalize it, to make it part of the body.

The gentleman certainly seems to know what he wants, the clerk muses—not once, but twice—as Scottie describes with a dressmaker's specificity the outfit he wants to purchase for Judy.

DIRECTOR'S NOTE, SCENE 133

What is a body but a tool?
In this case just a placeholder,

a cipher,
an empty space.

I have taken him out of my body,
placed him into yours where he can live again.

You possess me inside of you.

IV.

The Strange Case Of Maribel Dixon

"A lightning bolt is made entirely of error."
—Galway Kinnell

PREFACE: FRAGMENT FROM EDWARD DIXON'S THESIS MANUSCRIPT *MANIFESTATIONS OF METAPHYSICAL ENERGY AS BIOLOGICAL ENTITIES: SURVIVAL WITHIN THE GHOST-WORLD DIMENSION*, AS DISCOVERED BY GRADUATE STUDENT RESEARCHERS ARCHIVING HIS PAPERS (1921)

[PAGE MISSING]

. . . for this reason I refer to this dimension that (normally) lies outside our frame of perception "The Ghost-World" in coy allusion to the realm's determinate intangibility. There are no palpable entities within this further dimension and so, much like the ghost stories of our youth, all that exists in this "other world" are disembodied voices. Or—to put it plainly—language and its verbalization: the sound wave.

Communication between our dimension and the Ghost-World is rare at best. It seems that only through the intervention of some mechanical objects can actual connection be made. Because I isolated certain properties of the Ghost-World, I can firmly assert that the dimension can conduct forms of energy, among them what we commonly refer to as electricity.

I theorize that entry to the Ghost-World by inhabitants of our dimension is possible, although potentially life-threatening. On the following page you will see a rough schematic drawing of a machine I believe will translate the human body into . . .

[PAGE MISSING]

I. DOCUMENTATION OF EDWARD DIXON'S FIRST ATTEMPT TO REACH THE GHOST-WORLD: NOVEMBER, 1934

Once the design of the equipment was complete, Dixon moved his laboratory and his wife into an abandoned air hanger previously used to assemble general infantry units during the Great War. Despite Dixon's genius, the machinery required to complete the translation was large, metallic, full of switches and hundreds of whining gears. And what noise it made: Dixon could feel the workings of the machinery within his body as the large gears tore at each other; the smaller, more intricate parts—pieces Dixon pored over with his soldering gun for weeks at a time—pierced the air like the shrieks of cats skinned alive.

They were secluded enough that the ruckus caused by the lab had no witnesses other than Dixon and his wife.

Dixon's wife Maribel was the first test subject. A fellow physicist, Maribel was, one might say, distinguished—intelligent eyes, her blonde hair slowly giving itself over to a polite gray, the smile lines around her mouth both generous and unobtrusive. But she was sick, slowly dying of a cancer that would surely grow only more painful the longer her life wore on. Edward could sense in her a kind of dimming. He knew the Ghost-World was her only hope to survive the year.

It was a harrowing procedure. The telephone was then the Ghost-World's only known entry point. Dixon knew Maribel's body would first be decomposed into its individual molecules by the machinery, which then translated Maribel's body into corresponding bolts of energy that traveled through some copper wiring to a telephone receiver.

It was a risk, Maribel knew, going first. But what was love if not our first and most important risk? She would always love Edward. Her molecules refused to unknow him; her energy, she was sure, would remember to love him.

When Maribel entered the machine, feet first, and slowly slipped inside up to her neck, Dixon begged her to stop. But she was resolute. For her, there would be no Ghost-World—only this one, without the burden of her body to weigh her down.

Ia. ENTRY: EDWARD DIXON'S DIARY (OCTOBER 6, 1943)

A message from the Ghost-World: *be brave*. Imagine a room full of shoes, how much potential that is.

Or the room of car keys, the room of overstuffed messenger bags. The room of travel-sized soaps.

Everything piles up by category, discrete lists of things that take me to you.

To find you I'll need a fifth dimension, beyond space and time. I won't name it—what this is, how I get to you. How I was found again, rescued again, restored again.

The Ghost-World hasn't missed me. But I miss you.

1b. SHREDDED DOCUMENT RECOVERED FROM THE DIXON PAPERS, REASSEMBLED JANUARY 2006 (I)

In the dream
        the Ghost-World
                was our only world:

where we lived
        there was a bed
                there was a mirror

and each other
        doubled in glass—
                there's so much love

it takes bodies
        dark and duplicate
                to contain us in it

1c. ENTRY: EDWARD DIXON'S DIARY (APRIL 22, 1954)

Our voices connect in the Ghost-World and, overlapping, make the strange sinews our bodies cannot: a new sound unlike ourselves.

Our voices connect in the Ghost-World and in the overlap discover strange tones, secret tones. A secret message in our breath.

Our voices connect in the Ghost-World and the overlap of our words is eclipse: there is sound and the corona of sound, the fire that seals around it and glows.

Our voices connect in the Ghost-World and overlap, slip into each other as though we could kiss this way, divided by long stretches of land. The closest thing I have to your taste is the way you say *Good night*.

Our voices connect in the Ghost-World. Over the lap of invisible wires strung tower to tower, I am broken down into air. I am lighter than air.

Our voices connect in the Ghost-World. The overlap is all we have to give.

2. MARIBEL VANISHES, NOVEMBER 1934

In a flash of light and a deafening clanging of machinery, Maribel vanished.

The change was so immediate there was no witnessing the translation of her body into particles and then into energy. Like a solid bursting immediately into gas, she was first there and then not there.

Records of the incident are sketchy, but indications exist in Edward's diary from that period that his reaction to Maribel's disappearance was immediate and violent. And how couldn't it be: she was his love. To have love and to lose it is our only failure; to have love and destroy it, our only crime.

In a 1944 interview, Dixon claimed the experiment was a complete and total success. This record conflicts with a 1972 tapescript in which Dixon admits total failure and confesses to the unintentional murder of his wife Maribel. There is no conclusive evidence to either case, and so the strange disappearance of Maribel Dixon has never been fully or satisfactorily explained.

2a. SHREDDED DOCUMENT RECOVERED FROM THE DIXON PAPERS, REASSEMBLED JANUARY 2006 (2)

I tell you this is what physics is:

    our bodies in collision
    and the force of impact we accumulate over time

        In the Ghost-World we are just our voices,
        just waves

particles and nothing else

    The way our imagined kiss
    its heat

        made the memory of our faces sweat
        and our hands

dreamed sordid private lives

I tell you the Ghost-World
    does not observe verb tense and so what happens there

        happens continually
        and returns to occur again—

we can have   no future here

    In the real world
    there is a car

        the engine is idling
        and your hands are clutching the wheel

I tell you fire changes things

in ways we can't imagine
What burns

                                becomes alive. Your foot on the gas
                                is the perfect arsonist

2b. ENTRY: EDWARD DIXON'S DIARY (JULY 17, 1937)

There is no poverty of distance, for all we have is separation, distance, miles and maps; we have gasoline tanks, seaplanes and even once we had a transit tram—and there was also that time we walked together and held hands like nobody cared.

There is no poverty of reasons. Reasons are sticking their pointy noises from the soil all over the yard and each one smells like you. And I know the reasons will bloom into permissions at any moment.

And our imaginations are not poor. If I listed all the ways I have already experienced you in your absence I would be arrested for indecency. I would be arrested for gross negligence of propriety and I'm okay with that. This is not a poverty of freedom so they can take that from me. This is not a poverty of love so they can take that from me. This is not a poverty of future because nobody owns the future, not even God. Not even us.

3. EDWARD DIXON'S SUBSEQUENT ATTEMPTS TO REACH THE GHOST-WORLD WERE UNSUCCESSFUL

Over the next two decades, Edward Dixon devoted himself to locating Maribel in the Ghost-World in order to return her to our plane of existence, the physical world. The world of physical love.

There is no map of the Ghost-World. Since Dixon's experiments became part of the public record upon his court-determined death in 1974, cartographers have puzzled themselves over the location of the Ghost-World, its topography. No map withstands the Ghost-World's dizzying contradictions. And so, those who are lost there remain lost.

Among his papers and notes are several shredded documents carefully reconstructed by the graduate staff of this department to the best of their ability. Puzzling, they seem to be transcripts of a voice unlike Dixon's. Philip Harwood, Dixon's primary biographer, has theorized these documents are "automatic writings" resulting from the extensive drug and alcohol use of Dixon's later years. Scholars of Dixon's papers have not yet explained the significance of these items, although they number upward of 10,000 pieces.

Edward Dixon's air hanger and physiotranslator (as it became known) were destroyed by fire around the time the scientist himself disappeared. Fire marshals agree it was arson but no suspect was ever named and the investigation was left unsolved.

There are many mysteries surrounding the Dixon experiments and we have yet to draw any significant conclusions regarding the Ghost-World, about Maribel Dixon, and about the fateful machine that possibly turned human flesh into dynamic, non-corporeal energy.

Edward Dixon's body was never discovered and his death was ruled a suicide by the New York courts at the petition of his brother Michael Dixon.

3a. SHREDDED DOCUMENT RECOVERED FROM THE DIXON PAPERS, REASSEMBLED JANUARY 2006 (3)

To be shapeless

    is what you've given me

        I can't describe the form of your voice, its energy

            or the timbre of our love, which has its own noise

                I am in the dark

                    I am part of the dark

                        And yet, explain to me how it is

                          that only now

                              our voices have their own hands

                            their own needs

                      and make bodies out of sound

                  The complete body

has four hands, my love—

I am in your dark

I am waiting for you in this dark

and my voice has opened itself like a glove

3b. ENTRY: EDWARD DIXON'S DIARY (DECEMBER 14, 1960)

What happens when my voice goes out to you but you aren't there to hear it? I question the role of the ear in everything, in our love. Hearing isn't active, it's passive. It happens to you. I listen, I have intent, I wait for you by the phone.

This is and will ever be the one thing I crave to be told: *I'm here*. It means you are with me if not in person then at least in sound.

I imagine you in the sky like a rose quartz miming a dim star. You glow that way and have strange properties I don't understand. Either way, I can't hold you, but I gaze up where I think you might be and that is how I love you.

My poor body wishes it could hold you. Such a simple, plain need, touch is. And without it, how are we lovers? Divided between our bodies and ourselves something gets lost. I send out vibes to the Ghost-World like a little radar gun. They grow ever wider as they move and I hope, somehow, they capture you in their lariat pulse.

3c. SHREDDED DOCUMENT RECOVERED FROM THE DIXON PAPERS, REASSEMBLED JANUARY 2006 (4)

You couldn't stop
        believing in me—
faith is always
        invisible. It will not be proved true.
I remember the story of Pascal
        who said, *Believe in God, just in case*—
But that's not why
        you believe in me, why you
hear my voice
        and in an instant know where I am
even when a voice
        is all I am
all I can be
        all I will ever be
You say my body
        is a sound, not a thing, not a smell
I say my body is all wrong,
        but even then you hear it,
backwards, and you believe it.

4. EDWARD DIXON, THE RECLUSE

In interviews recorded after Edward's death, Edward's brother Michael Dixon commented on his sibling's highly eccentric and compulsive behaviors:

> One thing he was particularly strange about was the telephone. I remember calling to check on him one morning after he'd had an especially worrisome period when he dreamed constantly of Maribel. He picked up the phone and, with a desperation in his voice I never heard before or since, he whispered, "*Yes?*" I said, It's your brother. "Dammit!" he shouted into the phone. "Don't ever call this line." And he slammed the phone down. Well, I hardly knew what to make of that, so I went right over there. Edward hadn't showered for days, nor shaved in at least twice as long. His bathrobe was torn through with ragged holes. When I walked in the front door, he was clutching the receiver so tightly his hand was white and bloodless. He just sat there, pressing the index finger of his other hand onto the hookswitch over and over, pausing each time as if he were waiting to hear the dial tone. I'll never forget his face, how intent his expression was, as though if he pressed it enough, the phone would connect to God Himself....
>
> (Dixon Tapescripts #11-13, 1982)

4a. ENTRY: EDWARD DIXON'S DIARY (MAY 21, 1974)

How do you love a lightning bolt? The answer: you do it quickly, and once.

4b. DOCUMENT 729: SINGED FRAGMENT DISCOVERED NEAR SITE OF EDWARD DIXON'S BURNED LABORATORY, CA 1974

Now I see the truth—no hope to bring you back. They say lightning does not strike twice. It is true, it is true.

Your voice cannot contain me. My body cannot sustain you. We have come now to an impasse of disability. Each of us is broken and incomplete. I call to you, I call to you, I call to you.

The gears can be set in motion, the circumstance surrounding them can burn slowly while my body erupts into the violence you know. I remember the room of car keys. My voice is an arsonist for your love and everything smolders in preparation. There is the machine, there is love, there is travel. When I am gone the fire will keep me yours.

I will find you in the Ghost-World, in the dark—I would find you even if my hands were tied, my voice choked back—

4c. SHREDDED DOCUMENT RECOVERED FROM THE DIXON PAPERS, REASSEMBLED JANUARY 2006 (5)

If I asked you
where am I?

I know
you'd have little to say.

I am where
there is no *you*,

where I haven't seen
a lamppost

or a mirror
or a stack of nickels

in as long
as I can think of.

No matter how long
I may be vanished like this,

I will hear
the tires of your voice breaking gravel

to find me
even though

I will not be found.
If I asked you

where is my body?
It would not be in vain.

There is no riddle
more complex than us. Simply say,

You have no need for body,
I am filled with you already.

About the Author

Charles Jensen won the 2006 Frank O'Hara Chapbook Award for *Living Things*. *The Strange Case of Maribel Dixon* was recognized as a published finalist for the DIAGRAM/New Michigan Press Chapbook award the following year. A past recipient of an Artist's Project Grant from the Arizona Commission on the Arts, his poetry has appeared in *Bloom*, *Columbia Poetry Review*, *Copper Nickel*, *The Journal*, *New England Review*, *spork*, and *West Branch*. He holds an MFA in poetry from Arizona State University and is the founding editor of the online poetry magazine *LOCUSPOINT*, which explores creative work on a city-by-city basis. He serves as director of The Writer's Center, one of the nation's largest independent literary centers, and on the board of directors of the Arts & Humanities Council of Montgomery County. He lives in Maryland.

LaVergne, TN USA
09 October 2009
160340LV00002B